What's the best you
can do?

"What's the best you can do?"

First-hand Recollections of a
Second-hand Bookseller

Derek Rowlinson

Illustrated by Graham Kennedy

Clive Scoular

First published in March 2009

Publisher: Clive Scoular

© 2009 Derek Rowlinson

ISBN 978-0-9539601-6-3

Acknowledgements

Thank you to Clive Scoular for kindly volunteering to edit my jottings, and to Thomas Johnston for dealing with the typesetting and general layout. Thanks also to Graham Kennedy, a friend of 30 years standing, for agreeing to illustrate the book for me and to Mark Thompson for designing the cover. Finally, I would like to express gratitude to my wife, Hilary, who by rolling her eyes when I told her I was writing this, made me more determined to see it through to publication, just for badness!

For Hilary, James and Thomas

Preface

Over the years I've scorned so many vanity publications which had little or no literary merit.

Here is an opportunity for others to scorn mine.

Contents

Foreword

I first met Derek Rowlinson at one of those popular bookfairs that were all the rage some years ago. In those days I was new to the game of seeking out books on Ireland's history and was very much feeling my way. As I searched the shelves of books for sale I encountered this rather enigmatic bookdealer who clearly knew his stuff, although there was a certain brusqueness about him that didn't seem quite right. I just put it down to him having an off day, something which you will easily forgive him for when you read some of his recollections.

Happily, it took mere moments on that first meeting to see past that outward rough edge and to recognise the spark which was to lead to a lasting friendship. I quickly discovered that Derek was an incredibly kind and generous man. He had the knack of being able to take things rather seriously yet still was able to poke fun at them without even a hint of malice or antagonism. He told me stories that made me laugh out loud and which continued to make me chuckle as I recalled them later on. He is open, honest and dependable — all of which qualities I personally count highly in any friend or acquaintance.

This book of anecdotes from Derek's bookshop-owning days is a gem. Against the disruption of the 'Troubles' he has found the best, the worst and the most curious of people coming into his shops in Belfast and Bangor. To have been a second-hand bookseller during those times took extraordinary courage and perseverance. Yet even against this backdrop, or maybe because of it, here are stories that are out and out funny (and I defy you to hold back your laughter); others are poignant; yet more are just quirky; but all are true. They provide an insight not only into Derek's life as a second-hand bookseller and a man struggling to make ends meet in difficult times, but also into human behaviour in general. Within these brief snapshots into other people's lives you will recognise, and possibly identify with, the whole range of human characteristics and traits. But the constants throughout are Derek's wit, his love for his work and his ability to tell a good yarn.

Clive Scoular
February 2008

Introduction

I intended to write this book fifteen years ago and call it *First Impressions*, a very apposite title then, although perhaps a little obvious and hackneyed. I had even made a start to it, but quickly dropped the idea in the belief that nobody would be interested in reading it.

Had it not been for a series of chance circumstances leading to one of my anecdotes being broadcast on BBC Northern Ireland's *Days Like This* radio programme, I would not have given another thought to the book.

I was very surprised at the positive response to that broadcast and subsequently the story was one of a number selected to be made into an animation for local television. It went out on Tuesday 16 December 2008 at 10.45 pm on BBC1 Northern Ireland, and again the feedback was rewardingly favourable. This gave me the impetus to revisit the idea of writing a book.

My logic was that if people enjoyed that story then they might well enjoy some of the others I had to tell of my bookshop days. That logic may well prove to be false, but once I'd started writing I felt compelled to see it through to completion and have the book published, for better or worse.

My life has by no means been one of high adventure, and I have no pretensions to being a good writer, so I do not expect this volume of autobiographical jottings and anecdotes to make any best-seller lists, but hopefully some part of it will prove interesting and entertaining to a few.

I have generally found that from within the pages of even the most humble book I have been able to extract a few nuggets of useful information or gain a little amusement. I hope others may be able to do the same with mine.

Other second-hand booksellers at least should get a little entertainment value out of it. They will have shared many similar experiences and should find much with which to identify. They will know that the incidents I describe in many of the anecdotes are not exaggerated for effect, because they will have faced the same and even worse.

Finally, I have no desire to offend anyone with what I have written, so to avoid that possibility I have deliberately kept locations vague and changed names where appropriate.

How I Became a Second-hand Bookseller

In 1987 I was a 26 year old mature student studying for a business degree at university. This was my placement year and despite receiving the 'Dean's Letter' and being on course for first class honours, I was the only person in my year who hadn't been allocated a job by the end of the summer.

Then, at the eleventh hour, I received a call from the lecturer in charge of placements, who asked me to come to see him. He told me that he'd fixed me up with a job as manager of a filling station on the Crumlin Road in Belfast, where I'd be on a good wage and would receive free petrol. When I got there I discovered that the garage already had a manager, several years my junior, who handed me a brush and told me to sweep the forecourt. The wages were to be 90 pence an hour (a pittance even then) and the petrol wasn't to be discounted, never mind free. Besides that, I learned that previous tenants there had been shot dead so, on balance, I decided to give it a miss.

I hasten to add that it wasn't because I thought the work beneath me in any way, or that I was particularly afraid of getting shot at, but rather that I had a strong aversion to being taken for a mug.

A few days later I was in Smithfield Market trying to offload some of my books in order to raise a few shillings to keep me going for a day or two. I was disappointed in what the bookseller offered me, but took the opportunity of asking him had he any work going. He explained that he hardly earned enough to keep himself going, let alone pay someone else. I thanked him for his time and he pointed me in the direction of another second-hand bookshop in the city.

There I initially met with the same response when I asked for employment, but this time I persevered. I said that I'd work for nothing if the owner gave me a month's trial. Eventually he acceded and I began my career in the second-hand book trade the following morning.

The Bookshop

It was an old-fashioned, double-fronted shop, with a covered recess in the middle which tapered towards a glass-panelled door, and a little bell tinkled on entering.

In the windows was a miscellany of books, with covers curled or faded by the light of the sun. Each had a little hand-cut and hand-written price ticket, made from card and never quite square, which was attached to the book by a sliver of age-yellowed tape. Here and there lay the mortal remains of wasps and bluebottles in various stages of decomposition.

The shelves were made from bare, unvarnished wood, and evidently assembled by eye, so that scarcely one shelf ran parallel to another. The edges were often rough with splinters, and nails were visible where the horizontals had been sawed too short to meet the uprights. Some had collapsed under the weight of books and were propped up by the volumes on the shelf below.

A line of broken cardboard boxes, overflowing with a jumble of books, ran along the centre of the shop like a spine, largely hiding the dusty old mats on which they sat.

The counter was an old beaten-up wooden desk, with barely a square inch of its top surface visible between the precarious stacks of volumes, piled so high, and always threatening to collapse. Dotted about, half-buried in little niches, were pens and pencils (which doubled as stirring spoons), a knife, a rubber, elastic bands, a pot of glue, tea-stained mugs, and other tools of the trade.

Books which had parted company with their bindings had glue applied to the spines with the flat edge of a knife, then the two parts were reunited and clasped together with three elastic bands — top, middle and bottom. These were placed at the top of piles to dry out and bond before taking their place on the shelves amongst the serried ranks of more fortunate volumes.

The legs and sides of the desk were also obscured by boxes of books, one stacked on top of the other, waiting in turn to have their contents examined and priced. Only the barest necessary space was left to allow access, with a squeeze and careful navigation, to the tall, three-legged wooden stool, the seat of knowledge, from which business would be conducted.

The till was an old biscuit tin in the top right-hand drawer of the desk, which held the coins, whilst notes were generally secreted in different pockets about the person.

Getting Started

I left school (Methodist College, Belfast) in 1978 having failed my 'A' Levels due to a complete lack of interest. Subsequently, I had taken several jobs simply because they were there at the time and served their purpose in terms of generating an income for me. Even on deciding to go back to full-time education I had no idea what I wanted to do at the end of it all, and picked my subjects largely by eliminating all those that I definitely *didn't* want to do.

All that changed within my first week at that second-hand bookshop in Belfast. The physical and intellectual environment seemed to commune with my very soul, and I knew that the long search for a vocation was finally over, that I'd somehow come home.

As I was on a trial, I felt obliged to prove my worth, and I realised the only practical way of doing that was by increasing the sales revenue of the shop.

The bookseller held the belief that everyone should enjoy the pleasure of serendipity or, in other words, the books should be left completely unordered so that customers were more likely to stumble across something they liked by chance. Philosophically, I didn't disagree with him in this, but it was soon obvious that time was at a premium for most people visiting the shop, and having the books categorised would help them find what they wanted more quickly, thus increasing sales.

So, the first thing I did was to begin the process of organising the stock into categories, which helped familiarise me quickly with many different authors and publishers, past and present.

Whereas he didn't oppose me in this plan and, in fact, theoretically supported me in it, the bookseller just couldn't bring himself to actively participate, so continued to dump books randomly on the floor and on the shelves, almost as fast as I could sort them. Eventually, however, I did manage to get the stock sorted into broad categories and placed identifying stickers on each section.

The *Bookdealer*

On my first Thursday I was introduced to the *Bookdealer*, the main weekly trade magazine. In this was an editorial and articles about various aspects of the second-hand book trade, but the bulk of it was devoted to 'for sale' and 'wants' advertisements.

Here I saw another opportunity to increase turnover, and began scouring the shelves in earnest, with the intention of finding as many books as possible which matched the 'wants' ads.

This is how it worked. *Bookdealer* would send out a bundle of blank quotation slips on which the bookseller would record details of the books he or she had for offer to the advertisers, including condition, price, and postage and packaging charges. The bundle of completed slips would be posted back to the magazine, which then redistributed them to the appropriate bookdealers.

Then it was a question of waiting.

I found myself eagerly anticipating the arrival of the postman each day, wondering how successful my latest quotations might be. Advertisers would respond directly to the bookseller, so the bigger the bundle of letters the better. Some enclosed cheques with the order, whilst others preferred to pay on receipt. The latter was hardly ever a problem, as transactions within the book trade were largely based on trust, and defaulters were extremely rare.

Apart from the buzz I got from seeing the money come in, there was something romantic in the notion that books which had been read and cherished in this country were to find, through the medium of an unpretentious second-hand bookshop in Belfast, new readers and homes in other parts of the world.

Although it was a predominantly British trade journal, dealers from across the world would advertise in it, and it wasn't long before I became acquainted with international postal rates.

Sadly, the *Bookdealer* and other trade magazines did not long survive (at least in physical form) the advent of the Internet.

My Apprenticeship Ends

My year of apprenticeship passed in the blink of an eye, but because I had loved it, lived it and breathed it, I probably learned more in that year than in all of the previous years of my life put together.

I would spend my evenings perusing articles in the *Book and Magazine Collector*, reading novels on bookshops and booksellers, or studying books of bibliography. I learned to tell my quartos from my octavos, woodcuts from steel engravings, calf from morocco.

My efforts to improve the shop's trade had, after a while, been duly recognised, and the bookseller thenceforth paid me as much as he was able to afford.

But the time to return to university inevitably came, and I found myself reluctant to go. Logic dictated that I should finish what I'd started and not waste the two years I had already spent there, so back I went.

Unfortunately, I discovered that try as I might, I could not focus on my studies, and I was becoming increasingly bored and frustrated.

It was at this point that I formulated a plan and made the decision which determined the course of my life for the next twenty years.

During my placement year the bookseller had periodically made noises about wanting to be free of the shop, to work from home, selling only the rarest of books, as the bigger dealers did. So, I went to see him and suggested, trepidatiously, that I might buy him out.

To my great joy and relief the response was positive. All we had to do was settle on a deal which would suit us both.

We agreed on a figure of £10,000 for the stock and goodwill, although the fact that I had no money posed a bit of a problem. That was resolved by us agreeing that I pay him £200 each week for fifty weeks, by the end of which I would be the master of all I surveyed. He could hold on to the lease, which had a year to run, as security against me defaulting.

It couldn't have been better. I was getting a business without having to find the money up front (which I would have struggled to do) and he would receive regular income for a year whilst he built up his mail order and 'by appointment only' business.

Perfect.

Out on My Own

Much as I loved how the old shop had looked, I had to increase turnover substantially to meet my repayments, rent, and other costs, as well as provide for my wife and young son, so I invested the surplus of the first few weeks' takings into making 'improvements'.

I bought cheap, durable carpet from friends who were in the trade and removed the worn old mats and mountains of books which littered the floor. I bought in fresh planks of wood and rebuilt the shelves, measuring, cutting and assembling them carefully before adding a couple of coats of woodstain.

Knowing things would be tight that first year, and that the stock would run down dramatically, I made several wider racks at the front of the shop to display 'glossies', or large coffee-table type books. The beauty of this was that by showing these face out it only took a fraction of the books to fill the shelves, as opposed to filling them spine out — and, if anything, it increased sales rather than reduced them.

I cleaned out and carpeted the windows as well, taking time to dress them properly and present the books which were most likely to draw people in.

The old desk and till system remained.

On the subject of tills and taking money, it should be noted that no use was ever made of calculators or pen and paper. The cost of all transactions was computed by mental arithmetic alone, and this was often more involved than one might think.

I inherited a system of exchange whereby customers would return books they had read and receive credit against what they took out. Often ten to twenty books were taken out at a time and I, like my predecessor, had to rapidly sum the total of the prices in my head — and they weren't all nice, easy round numbers — then deduct half the value of their returns from that.

Naturally, there were always those who would try to abuse the exchange system. The understanding was that I would take back what had been bought from me, but some people would present me with tat that they'd picked up elsewhere and swear sincerely that it was from my shop. But prices were always marked inside the books in pencil and each bookseller's 'handwriting' was easily identifiable.

When I later opened a shop in Bangor, a friend asked me if I would be prepared to give his daughter a part-time job so that she could earn a little extra cash. She was a high-flying 'A' Level pupil at a local grammar school and went on to become a well-paid professional in her chosen scientific career, yet was entirely unable to cope with the most simple exchange without resort to pen and paper.

Buy-ins too required mental dexterity. I could be presented with a hundred or more books at a time and have to cumulatively add my calculated value of each whilst perhaps simultaneously conducting a conversation or dealing with several interruptions.

A more physical form of discipline was keeping the shop open six days a week, no matter what. I just couldn't afford to be ill, so the show went on at all costs. I remember having a nasty dose of gastro-enteritis during that time, and fitting in visits to the powder room between serving customers proved quite a challenge.

I kept the shop open all that first year without closing one day through illness or any other reason, though I could certainly have done with the break at times.

By the end of the year I had met the rent on time, paid off the owner, and managed to eke out a living. When I submitted my accounts to the accountant, he looked at me accusingly and said — "You can't possibly tell me that *this* is what you lived on?" I remember being mighty angry at the time because *that* was exactly what I had lived on.

People, especially well-paid professionals, often don't realise what frugal lives others have to lead. It was often an erroneous assumption that because I ran a shop, had my own business, I was well-off financially. Not true. In fact, I don't recall ever meeting a wealthy second-hand bookshop owner — at least not one with a family, who depended on the shop entirely. Some single men I knew didn't have to struggle so hard, but they were by no means in the higher income tax brackets and were unlikely to ever make the world's richest people lists.

To make a living as a professional second-hand bookseller, with no other source of income, is tough. I have done it now for more than twenty years and don't recall a period of respite from the constant struggle to meet bills. It has meant living a life of relative penury, with none of the indulgences that most others in our society have enjoyed over the same period. No holidays. No luxuries. Clothes and household furniture have all been either bought second-hand or donated, and the contents of my vehicle fuel tanks have generally been more valuable than the cars themselves.

The foregoing is not a complaint or plea for sympathy, but rather a part description of a way of life concomitant with the path I chose. Thankfully, I have never really wanted 'things', other than my books. Still, I could have done without the worry of meeting all those bills over the years.

At the same time, I regard myself as fortunate to have lived in such an affluent society where I've wanted for no essentials. I remind myself that others in the world have died of hunger during the same period.

Towards the end of that first year in business I had another bridge to cross. I had to persuade the landlord to allow me to take over the tenancy of the building, and I approached him on the matter. I had paid him on time and without problem at the beginning of each quarter, yet he was strangely non-committal. I then discovered through the grapevine that he had someone else lined up to take over the shop, someone with what he obviously regarded as a more respectable or prestigious occupation.

As I entered the final weeks of the existing tenancy agreement, I still had not heard word from him one way or another. Then I discovered that the landlord's preferred tenant had pulled out at the eleventh hour, and shortly afterwards he was on the phone to me saying that the lease was mine if I wanted it.

"Too late," I said. "I've just enlisted in Foreign Legion."

I could not trust and did not want to do business with such a slippery customer, so a van was hired and the shop emptied and swept clean overnight.

Then began a series of short peregrinations around Belfast, Bangor, and even Blackpool in England, before settling for a small shop in a Bangor side-street.

What follows is an account of some of the experiences I had, mostly humorous, but some sad, in the various shops I worked in over the years.

I learned a great deal about books during my shop years, but learned even more about human psychology and the nature of man.

One thing I would add is that before I began in the book business I found it difficult to be overtly rude to people. A few months on my own in a second-hand bookshop in the middle of Belfast soon cured me of that. And lest any of you are inclined to judge me harshly on my behaviour in any of the following anecdotes, I would like to suggest that had you travelled the same road, you might have arrived at the same destination!

Ask a Silly Question

My first shop in Belfast was in quite an old building, but I had absolutely no idea of even its most recent history, until one day a woman passed under the shop sign at the front, walked between the two display windows, through the door, past the ranks of coffee-table volumes at the front, approached the desk and over a mountain of books asked:

"Is this not a grocery shop any more?"

Another lady came in to ask me if I fixed cassette recorders. Presumably my oversight in not having a 'We do not fix cassette recorders' notice in the window was what prompted her to enquire.

One man asked — "Do you have any books on bomb-making?"

This was *Belfast* in the middle of the 'Troubles.'

He correctly read the expression on my face as he quickly waved his hand to and fro, and added by way of reassurance:

"No, no, it's not for *me*…it's for my son's school project."

I don't know what sort of school his son went to, but bomb-making definitely hadn't been on my Chemistry curriculum.

There were a number of common questions for which I developed standard responses. Whenever someone asked 'Do you buy books or just sell them?' I would always reply that I just sold them. My theory was that anyone who asked that question was unlikely to be offering literature of great merit.

To the few who were perceptive enough to follow up by asking 'Where do you get your books from then?' I would describe the annual mystery delivery, accompanied by the sound of sleigh bells, every 25th of December.

Having a whopping great 'Bookshop' sign above the door, and price stickers on every display book, didn't deter some people from asking 'Is this a library?'

'Yes' was my standard reply to that one.

"How does it work?" one chap asked.

"Well, you pick the books that you like, leave a deposit with me and, unlike other libraries, here you get to *keep* them."

Another perennial was 'Have you read all these?'

"Yes," I would say. "And I particularly enjoyed the *Mark III Ford Cortina Maintenance Manual* which had a fabulous plot and some terrific illustrations."

I won't go into the practical difficulties that booksellers would face if they could only replenish shelves with books they'd read, but even speed-readers would find the task more than somewhat difficult.

'How much do you pay for a book?' was another regular enquiry which made my heart sink. The underlying assumption was that all books are the same and should therefore be treated accordingly, whereas in truth all books are equal, but some are more equal than others.

It is perhaps one of the more forgivable silly questions, but it always amused me to think that I might get away with paying the same for a Mills & Boon romance novel as an original Shakespeare folio.

At times I confess that I was unduly flippant with those who didn't deserve it, as when a schoolboy from the Royal Belfast Academical Institution came into the shop during one lunch hour and said he was looking for *Julius Caesar*, to which I replied — "I'm sorry, son, he doesn't work here any more."

General Ignorance

We are all ignorant to some degree, it is simply a case of relativity.

Most people will have exposed their ignorance in some matters over the course of life, only to cringe with embarrassment on later discovering their faux pas.

In my first weeks responding to 'wants' ads in the *Bookdealer* magazine I offered a biography of the actress Liz Taylor to a dealer who requested quotations for 'books by or about' Elizabeth Taylor. I was completely unaware at the time of the well-known British authoress of the same name.

Thankfully I avoided making the same mistake with the actor Richard Burton who also has a famous literary namesake.

Another potential pitfall for neophytes of the book trade is with Winston Churchill. I narrowly escaped quoting books by the revered British Prime Minister to someone who actually wanted the works of the famous American novelist called Winston Churchill. The two men also happened to be contemporaries.

Lack of knowledge is different entirely to lack of thought and general stupidity, the former being easily forgivable in my eyes, the latter less so.

The point is, none of us knows everything, and although I found customers' unwitting blunders rather amusing, I did not disdain them unless they were accompanied by arrogance or rudeness.

Many who came through the door had never quite managed to come to grips with the concept of inflation, or believed that the second-hand book trade was somehow exempt from it, and this is why prices had to be clipped from the inside flaps of dustjackets and erased from the back covers of the older paperbacks. It was a disagreeable, but necessary practice — disagreeable because it was minor vandalism, but necessary in order to avoid constant debate and dispute. Part of the true bookseller's credo was to keep a book as close to its original state as possible, so it went against the grain to take scissors or pen to even the most humble tome. To do it to a collectible volume would constitute sacrilege, so many of these never made it to the shelves, but were sold directly to knowledgeable clients or through specialist magazines.

There were some older books, however, of no significant value, for which you were obliged to leave yourself open to attack. These had the original publication date and price printed on the front cover, and to deface a front cover was also regarded as a step too far, so the current price was pencilled inside, and the book put on sale in the hope that someone with at least a rudimentary grasp of economic theory would get to it first. Unfortunately, that wasn't always the case.

Having just put out a box of old sheet music books at a pound a piece, a lady lifted one and asked me accusingly:

"How can you charge a *pound* for this when it was only *sixpence* new?"

"Yes, but that was *6d*, and in *1886*," I pointed out.

She stared at me blankly, and I realised that I may as well have sung 'Hey Diddle Diddle, the Cat and the Fiddle' for all the effect it had on her.

"Okay," I said, "if you've got a thruppenny piece in your pocket, you can have it for that."

She didn't, and she left the shop no wiser than when she'd come in.

A chap came in one day and asked me for a copy of *David Copperfield*, so I plucked one from the shelves and handed it to him.

He quickly turned it over in his hands before declaring — "No, that's not it!"

"So, correct me if I'm wrong, but you're looking for the *other* David Copperfield by the *other* Charles Dickens, is that it?" I asked facetiously.

"Yes," he replied.

"Well, I'm sorry," I said, "but I don't have that particular title in stock at the moment."

Coming up to Christmas I overheard one woman ask her friend in a broad Belfast accent "What d'ye want to buy him that for? Sure he's already got a book."

There were people who only ever frequented bookshops in order to buy a gift for someone else and had no means of assessing the value of a book other than by price.

One well-dressed lady spent some time examining a late nineteenth century volume in a beautifully decorated cloth binding before coming to the counter and asking — "Could I have this, please?"

I looked at the pencilled price on the flyleaf and said — "That'll be six pounds."

"Oh!" she said in a disappointed tone, "I thought it was sixty," and with that she replaced the book on its shelf and left the shop.

A woman came into the shop with her teenage son and asked for a copy of *1984*.

"It's by George Orwell, you know," she added haughtily.

"Oh," I replied. "I thought it was by Eric Blair." (Orwell's real name).

"No, I *assure* you that it was written by *George Orwell*."

I got up from behind the counter to have a look, but before I'd even managed to take two steps she announced:

"You don't appear to have one."

I marvelled at her ability to scan every shelf in the bookshop so quickly and without even turning her head, but suspected I had a Penguin edition, so persevered in the search in my own plodding way.

A moment later I produced a copy and handed it to her. She, in turn, passed it to her son, who proceeded to examine the front and back cover before asking — "Is this the up-to-date version?"

I stood dumbfounded for a few seconds, hardly knowing how to respond.

"Yes," was the best I could manage.

Another woman came into the shop one day and asked me where I kept my Edna Blayton books. Now, I prided myself on my knowledge of authors, but this was a name which meant nothing to me.

"I'm sorry," I said, "I'm afraid that I've never heard of her."

"Edna Blayton!" she exclaimed incredulously. "The famous children's author?"

"No, I'm sorry," I repeated rather shamefacedly, "I don't recall ever having her books."

The lady left with a 'call-yourself-a-bookseller' look on her face
and I stood for a while racking my brains to see if something
might come back to me from within the deeper recesses of my
mind.

A few moments later I started to chuckle as the penny finally
dropped.

Rudeness

Until I ran my own shop I had no idea how incredibly rude and inconsiderate some people could be.

Chewing gum chewers had no reservations about disposing of their gum on the shelves, and some aberrant smokers thought nothing of dropping their cigarettes on the carpet and extinguishing them with a shuffle of the foot.

Then there were the people who would take a book from the shelves, have a look through, then just drop it on the floor and walk out.

One little bulldog-like man used to do it on a regular basis, and when he wasn't in the shop raising my blood pressure, he could be seen passing the window to give me a Churchillian victory salute — only with the hand reversed, and a little up and down movement added for good measure.

There were also those whose sole purpose in coming through the door was apparently to criticise.

One lady made a habit of coming in and addressing derogatory remarks about the shop to whichever sidekick she had with her on the day, although it was obvious to whom the comments were really directed.

With her smart clothes, fake accent, and a face which would curdle milk, she obviously held herself in the highest esteem, and my guess would be that she was the worst kind of know-nothing schoolteacher.

Eventually, I reached the point where I could take her no more. She came in one day with a tall, well-built man, whom I took to be her husband, and began her usual verbal assault on the shop, all for my benefit.

"You know," she announced, "I have never really managed to understand the layout of this shop — it's awfully confusing."

Her husband did not respond as she punctuated her sham browsing with one acid remark after another.

When I sensed that they were about to leave, I got up from behind the counter and put myself between them and the door.

"Can you explain to me why my shop should be laid out differently to any other bookshop and why, if it causes you so much grief, do you keep coming back?" I demanded of her.

There was a dead silence as she gaped back at me in shock. Momentarily, I feared that her husband might assault me but, instead, he turned to her and barked — "Well, can you?"

I could hear his raised voice the length of the street until they finally disappeared out of earshot.

She did not grace the shop with her presence again.

Thieves

I had to be on constant alert for the many and varied thieves doing the rounds.

There were those like 'Tea Cosy', so called because of the woolly hat he wore, who were regular hunters for books they could steal from one shop and then attempt to sell to another.

Every time Tea Cosy was in with me I tried not to take my eyes off him for a second, but followed him around and always kept the view between him and the shelves in my line of sight. Even when taking a sale or handling an enquiry I attempted to watch him unblinkingly.

Quite probably he was successful in his mission at least once when I was momentarily distracted but, if he was, he'd been made to work for it.

Others were more interested in taking the money and would

work in pairs. One would come in and try to lure me to the far end of the shop with an enquiry, whilst the other loitered at the door, ready to snatch the takings from the desk.

Naturally, I didn't move from my seat, but always suggested that the decoy should bring his enquiry to me, so the contents of the biscuit tin remained guarded.

Yet others seemed to be in it for the challenge more than anything.

I remember putting a new biography of T. E. Lawrence in the window, then a chap coming in and looking through it. When he moved away from the window I saw that the biography was missing and another book had been placed where it had been.

The thief soon became aware of me following him and turned to ask cockily — "Do you have any Agatha Christie books?"

He knew I knew, but just didn't care.

"No," I replied.

"Do you want to buy some?" he asked.

"No," I said, "but I wouldn't mind a biography of T. E.

Lawrence — and, by the way, where's the one you were looking at in the window?"

He pointed to an entirely different book.

Every time I tried to peer into his jacket from the top, he would turn away, and I'd manoeuvre in front of him again for another try, so that we both ended up doing a little ballroom dance around the shop.

Eventually I just lost patience and ripped his zipper jacket open, grabbed the book, and told him that I really ought to kick him up and down the shop for what he'd done.

I ejected him through the door by applying my knee to his posterior, which elicited the indignant response — "Excuse me, you can't treat me like this — I'm calling the police!"

"Be my guest," I said. "You know where to find me."

But oddly, I never saw or heard from him again.

Time-Wasters

Through experience I learned to judge with reasonable accuracy who were genuine book browsers and who weren't. It all came down to a combination of factors, like the way they walked about the shop, how they looked at the shelves and handled the books, and what they asked.

Money-jinglers, for example, never bought a thing. They liked to pretend that they had some purpose in the shop by turning their heads in different directions and rattling the small change in their pockets, but time-wasting was what they were really all about.

Suspected time-wasters were always open game as far as I was concerned.

One such suspect turned to me with a book in his hand and asked:

"Can you tell me what this is about?"

"Sorry," I said, "I can't read."

"You can't read?" he asked in astonishment.

"No."

For a moment he was speechless as he turned the matter over in his mind, then, intrigued, he asked:

"But if you can't read, how do you know where the books should go — I mean, like categories and that?"

"Well," I explained, "if they have pictures on the front then that gives me a pretty good idea, otherwise I just ask whoever's in the shop at the time."

He cogitated a while longer before asking:

"And how do you know what to charge people?"

"I'm not *stupid*," I snapped back with feigned indignation. "I know my numbers and can *count*. It's just words I have difficulty with."

By this stage he had swallowed the bait hook, line and sinker, and was obviously itching to get away to tell the world of his encounter with the illiterate bookseller.

As he made his way to the door, I held a book towards him and asked:

"Before you leave, would you mind telling me where this should go?"

One impeccably dressed, well-groomed gentleman spent some time browsing in the shop before informing me, in polished tones, of his particular book quest:

"I'm looking for a copy of a book called *The Frogmen*, which was written by Waldron and Gleeson, and published by Pan Books in 1954."

It so happened that I had an unusually pristine copy of that very title sitting on a shelf immediately behind my head, but something about him had triggered warning signals in my brain, so I simply replied — "Yes, I think I've heard of that."

He browsed a little longer before turning to me and nodding a 'thank you', then made his way to the door.

But I wasn't going to allow him to escape so easily.

Just as he was about to exit, I hastily plucked *The Frogmen* from the shelves, held it up to him and said:

"Excuse me, is this the book you are looking for?"

As I suspected, he wasn't entirely overjoyed at the find, but felt obliged to return to the counter.

I handed the book to him, and he examined it for a moment before saying:

"Yes, that's the one — how much is it?"

"Sixty pence," I said.

He then went through the pantomime of patting his trouser pockets with the palms of his hands:

"I don't appear to have any cash on me," he said. "I'll just nip out to the service till at the top of the street and be right back."

Needless to say, I never saw him again.

My nose for sniffing out time-wasters was not infallible, however.

A man once asked me for a title which I felt sure I'd seen recently, so I began scrutinising the shelves one by one until I'd covered the whole shop, but with no success. I asked him if he could bear with me a moment whilst I went to the storeroom to have a look, and there I proceeded to empty umpteen boxes of books in search of the one he wanted, until eventually I had to admit defeat and return to the shop empty-handed.

"I'm sorry," I said, "I feel sure I have a copy somewhere, but I just can't put my hands on it."

"Not to worry," he replied unconcernedly, "I have no money anyway."

People asking for books that they didn't really want was by no means unusual. On a number of occasions when I produced what people had asked me for, the reply was:

"It's good to know you have it in stock."

Some time-wasters were regular visitors.

The 'Clock Man' had been through the door countless times, ostensibly looking for books on horology, but no matter what I produced, he either already had it or it wasn't what he wanted.

I came to the conclusion that if I stocked every clock book ever published, I still wouldn't get a sale.

This man was obviously using the shop as a place to take shelter and kill time whilst he was waiting on something or someone else.

One morning I spotted him in the distance as he made his way towards the shop, and I just wasn't in the mood to have him about me.

The shop was empty at the time, so I got up and locked the door, then returned to my seat and proceeded to read a book.

I heard him try the door several times, but didn't look up. Then he knocked gently. I still didn't look up. The knocking got louder and louder until eventually I could ignore it no longer.

I went to the door and shouted through the glass — "Sorry, we're closed for lunch."

He pointed to his watch and shouted back, "But it's only 10 o'clock!"

"It's an early lunch!" was my riposte.

He didn't take the hint, but continued to visit the shop as regular as clockwork, if you pardon the pun, without ever managing to part with a penny.

Years later I saw him at an auction, bidding furiously for and buying a book which had sat on my shelves at a fifth of the price.

I came to sorely regret harassing one regular non-buyer.

He was one of a type of wee Belfast man who has all but disappeared now — a raincoat wearer who clicked and sparked about in metal-studded Oxford shoes (the ones which curled up at the toes) and had his hair slicked back with a gallon of oil.

This man had been in and out of the shop for months on end without managing to find anything worth buying, despite the fact that there were thousands of books on the shelves and fresh stock was coming in all the time. He never looked at or spoke to me on the way in, and never said so much as a 'thank you' on the way out.

One afternoon, after suffering my daily dose of abuse and having scarcely taken a farthing, he crept through the door as usual without even acknowledging my presence, and began to potter about the shop.

'Right!' I thought. 'That's it! I'm going to get rid of this guy once and for all'. So I got up from behind the counter and started to follow him around. Wherever he went, I went, and I stuck so close that he must have felt my breath on the back of his neck.

Then he paused at one point, lifted a book from the shelves, and began to leaf through the pages.

'Okay,' I said to myself, already slightly regretting my intimidatory tactic, 'let's just see what happens here.' And with that I took myself off and sat behind the counter again, watching.

He stood there for a while longer, just flicking through the book, then suddenly turned as though he'd reached a decision and made his way towards me.

Silently, he placed the book on the counter and slowly slid it across to me with his fingertips.

The title was *Loneliness*.

He handed me a pound and I gave him his change without a word exchanged between us.

As he opened the door to leave I said "goodbye" but got no response.

That was the last I saw of that poor wee Belfast man.

Meanness

A clergyman handed me a bag of books, saying — "These are probably too good for you, but have a look anyway." He wandered off to browse the shelves whilst I looked through his offerings. As it turned out, the bag would have been worth more than its contents.

He came back to the counter with four hardback religious books in his hand.

"Well?" he asked.

"You were quite right," I said, "these *are* far too good for here. You'd be well-advised to take them to the antiquarian bookshop on the Dublin Road."

"I thought as much," he replied. "So, tell me, how much do I owe you for these?"

He handed me the four books and I totted up the prices.

"Three pounds twenty-five," I said.

He dug deep into his pocket and fished out a fistful of coins, then started counting coppers into the palm of my hand. When he got to £1.50 he paused and asked — "Will that do you?"

"No," I said, "keep going."

He stopped again at £2 and asked — "Is that enough now?"

"No, you're alright," I replied, "you've a bit to go yet."

He continued to pause at every twenty-five pence after that, asking the same question and getting the same answer, until I eventually managed to get the whole three pounds twenty-five in my hand — all in coppers.

"You really ought to have a much larger religious section," he suggested as he was about to leave. "It would certainly be very popular."

"Actually, I'm considering disposing of that section altogether," I said, "as I find the clientele for those books too ridiculously mean for words."

A Jaguar pulled up outside the shop one afternoon, and a smartly dressed man in his early thirties got out and came into the shop with three paperback thrillers in his hand.

"Are these of any interest to you?" he asked.

They were recent, clean and reasonably sellable, so I said — "I could give you two pounds for them."

"Could you not make that two-ten?" he ventured.

On balance I decided that my need of the ten pence was probably greater than his.

I shall never forget the woman who stood at the bookshop window with a Chinese carry-out in one hand and armful of video rentals in the other, whilst her little daughter pointed at a fifty pence children's book I had on display.

"We haven't got money to waste on *that*," she told the girl peevishly, and shooed her along.

Meanness wasn't entirely the preserve of customers. Booksellers too could be somewhat mean in their dealings. Some, in fact, were very masters in the art of niggardliness.

Quite a few dealers came through my doors over the years in search of stock, and benefited from generous discounts of up to 50%, depending on how much they bought. The accepted norm for trade discount was only 10%.

The liberal discounts weren't just applied to help my cash flow, but because I understood that these fellow booksellers had to make a living as well, and I knew how tough that was to do.

Several dealers visited the shop on a regular basis to take advantage of the low rates they were charged, and jolly affable and grateful they appeared too. However, I discovered in due course that some weren't quite grateful enough to consider any degree of reciprocation.

I was sitting in my Bangor shop one afternoon when a shopkeeper from a few doors down, with whom I was friendly, came in and asked me would I take him to the casualty department in a nearby town, as he had injured his hand. I shut up shop and duly drove him there.

The queue at the hospital was pretty lengthy that day and it was obvious that my friend would be waiting quite some time before being seen, so I asked him if he'd mind me wandering into the town to have a browse round the second-hand bookshop there.

I knew the owner of that shop to be a man called, let's say 'Wally', as he had been a long-time beneficiary of discount from my shops. In fact, only a week or so previously I had contacted him to offer some pristine paperback novels I'd acquired as a job-lot, there being too many for my needs at that time. He and his wife came over to Bangor and took what they wanted at cost price.

I wasn't sure where the shop was as I'd never been to it or any of Wally's shops before. When I did find it, I entered to find his wife in charge.

As I looked about I began to spot books which I wanted to buy, but had left Bangor in a rush and without anticipating that I'd need cash, so had none on me.

I explained the situation to Wally's wife and asked her if she was happy enough with a cheque, but she very curtly told me that she wasn't.

I thought for a moment that she hadn't recognised me, didn't know who I was, and that it was all a bit of a misunderstanding, but I was soon disillusioned of that.

By this stage I was both insulted and becoming angry, but assumed that the situation might be remedied if the owner was consulted.

"Are you able to get in touch with Wally?" I suggested.

"No!" was all the reply I got.

Now, you may wonder why I didn't immediately leave the shop in high dudgeon and disgust at this treatment, but I had my reasons.

I spent a bit of time hunting around in the upstairs part of the shop and, although I'd just been told that the owner was uncontactable, when I came back down his charming partner snarlingly informed me:

"I've just spoken to Wally and he says it's cash or nothing."

"Okay," I said with a smile. "No problem."

I went back to the hospital, asked my friend to lend me £20 until we got back to Bangor, returned to the bookshop, quickly plucked five books from the shelves and presented them to Her Sweetness at the counter.

She totted them up and asked me for £18, which was the full price without a penny discount.

Normally I did not ask for discount if a bookseller wasn't prepared to offer it voluntarily, but in this case I virtually insisted upon it and was begrudgingly given 10%.

One of those books was a very good copy of an Arthur Rackham first edition, a highly collectible illustrator, which they had on sale for a fiver and I resold the same week for £150.

I made a good few quid from the others too.

Wally and his wife's Achilles' heel was that their love of money wasn't matched by their knowledge of books.

On my first visit to another local bookseller, let's call this one 'Tarquin', who had also regularly availed himself of my generous trade discounts, I managed to find a handful of books which interested me.

Buying from Tarquin in order to resell was rendered a little more difficult by the fact that instead of the normal trade practice of marking prices in pencil, he would write them in pen.

There were two theories doing the rounds as to why he did this. First, some were inclined to believe that he couldn't bear the thought of another bookseller making any profit from him, and would therefore discourage them by this means. The price could not be easily erased for a 'mark-up' and many booksellers were disinclined to disfigure a book by clipping the corner of a page to remove the pen price altogether.

The other theory was that he was paranoid with the thought that customers might come in with their own pencils and erasers and secretly mark his prices down before coming to pay for them.

He also had a habit of 'protecting' the edges of his books with sellotape, which actually destroyed them as far as book collectors were concerned.

As I waited for him to complete a transaction with another customer, he leaned to one side of her and asked me very nicely if I'd mind running to the bank for him as he was out of change.

I hurried down to the nearest bank with the notes he had given me, exchanged them for coins, and ran back to the shop as quickly as I could.

When he finished his transaction with the woman he'd kept waiting for her change, I handed him my books and he totalled them up.

"Fifteen pounds, five pence," he said sweetly. "But call it fifteen."

He delivered the blow so well and with such apparent conviction in his own bounty, that all I could do — without appearing petty — was to hold my tongue and admire his artistry.

Church sales were not my normal stomping ground in search of stock, but Tarquin was a seasoned veteran and took them very seriously.

I once went along to one with a friend and got great amusement from Tarquin's agitation at being behind us in the queue. It was very unlike him not to be first in line, and it would not have pleased him.

When the doors were opened, my companion and I made our way to a table of books and began browsing through them. As I stood with one in my hand, an arm flashed over my shoulder and snatched it from my grasp.

"That's funny," I said, turning to my friend, "I could have sworn I had a book in my hand a moment ago — and now it's gone!"

As quickly as it had disappeared it was plonked back into my hand, again from over my shoulder, and without a word of explanation.

I suppose whoever took it discovered that it was not of great interest to them after all, and thought the only polite thing to do would be to replace it.

I have heard it said that Tarquin employed some rather morally dubious tactics at church sales.

People have told me that he would apply his forearm to a table of books and quickly shovel them into boxes before anyone else had a chance to look at them, then put the boxes to one side for himself.

This would apparently allow him to sort through the books at his leisure without any competition or interference, and that he'd afterwards simply throw back what he didn't want to keep.

This is what I have heard, but I'm inclined to believe that it's too outrageous to be considered true.

The Mystery Donor

Unfortunately I am not in a position to regale you with a plethora of tales of generosity associated with my bookshop days. There is, however, one act of kindness which I will never forget and certainly bears telling.

I was sitting in the shop one day when a young woman in her early twenties came in and asked if I was Derek.

"Yes," I replied. "Why?"

She handed me an envelope and said — "I was asked to give you this."

I opened it immediately and found five twenty-pound notes inside.

"Hold on a second," I called to the girl as she was about to disappear through the door. "Who gave you this?"

"A woman."

"Who was she?" I asked.

"I don't know," she answered. "I've never seen her before."

The girl explained that she had simply been walking down the road on her way home when a middle-aged lady had stopped her and asked would she go into the bookshop to give me the envelope.

"Could you point her out to me?" I asked.

By the time we got outside there was not a soul to be seen on the street in any direction.

To this day I do not know the identity of that kind donor, but whoever it was must have been well aware of my straitened circumstances.

One of the 'suspects' that came to mind at the time was a lovely lady called Betty who would have been in her early fifties then, I think.

Betty came to Bangor once or twice a week from Donaghadee to do her shopping, and would come in to exchange a few books to keep her in reading material.

It was always a pleasure to see her come through the door as her face just radiated kindness and warmth. She often wore a brightly coloured beret which suited her personality very well.

I only ever charged Betty a token amount for her exchanges as I saw her more as a friend than a customer, but I remember her challenging me on this one day.

"Don't worry about it," I told her.

But knowing Betty, she probably did.

The shop was not generating enough revenue on its own to cover my living expenses, so I had started doing milk rounds at night to make up the shortfall. The shop was open Monday to Saturday and I was doing milk deliveries seven nights a week, so had little time for socialising, but I do remember once going to Betty's house in Donaghadee, seeing her garden (in which she took great delight) and having tea with her husband and mother. Betty and her husband also came to see us on a number of occasions at our wee terraced house in Bangor.

I remember her telling me that they'd decided to move to Bangor to be closer to the amenities it had to offer, and when they'd bought the new house she gave me the address.

I didn't see them for a few months, but assumed that they were busy with the move and settling in.

Coming up to Christmas I took a detour from the milk round I was on and drove to their new address in the early hours of the morning. I left a pint of milk on their doorstep with a note placed under the bottle wishing them a merry Christmas in their new home.

I thought it would give them a bit of a surprise and a laugh, and that they'd be in touch shortly, but I didn't hear a peep for some weeks after that.

Then one evening I got a telephone call from Betty's husband to tell me that she was dead. She had suffered a fatal asthma attack.

I remember being in a state of total disbelief and it was several minutes into the conversation before I accepted that it was true.

Subsequently the story was to become even more sadly tragic, but that is not for the pages of this book.

I can never know now for certain that the mystery donor was Betty but, irrespective of that, I offer these few pages as a worthy memorial to a kindly soul who is never far from my thoughts.

It just goes to show how one act of kindness can greatly outweigh countless others of a selfish nature in the impact and impression it can leave on a life.

Buying Books

Buying in books was the most pleasurable part of the job for me. There was always a sense of anticipation as to what I might find in a bag, a box, or on the shelves in a house.

The process wasn't without its drawbacks and pitfalls, however. Many sellers assumed that I would do my utmost to get the books for as little as possible and not pay them their true worth. Conversely, I had to be on my guard against all the tricks and pressures applied against me to buy what I didn't want or pay more than I ought.

Whatever shortcomings the Ulster Defence Association may have had as a paramilitary organisation, when it came to selling their publication, the *Ulster* magazine, their marketing technique couldn't be faulted.

A spokesman would come in with a bundle of the magazines under his arm, whilst four burly non-churchgoers would line up behind him.

"*Ulster?*" the spokesman would grunt.

"Why, certainly," I would reply. "I'd be only too delighted!"

There was also a chap who came in each week to collect for a loyalist prisoners' association. This was understood to be 'window money,' *i.e.* you paid it if you wanted to keep your windows.

Sometimes he would inform me that as he was off the following week it would be 'double' that day, so I was obliged to drop twice as many francs and pesetas into the collection box as normal. Foreign currency coins somehow managed to escape my eye and find their way into the biscuit tin, and there was no other practical means of getting rid of them.

On a number of occasions this man would turn up and apologise profusely for not having been in the previous week, explaining that he'd been too drunk to make it. The poor soul was under the impression that he'd somehow let me down.

Another less effective sales technique was employed by a young woman who came rushing in one day and thrust a bag of books into my hands.

"How much will you give me for these?" she asked impatiently.

They were all cheap, second-rate paperback romance novels — dog-eared, creased, yellowed with age, and entirely unsellable.

"Apologies," I said, "but I'm afraid I couldn't give you anything for them.

"But you don't understand," she replied desperately, "you *have* to buy them — I've got a taxi waiting outside and I don't have the fare!"

A little girl of about eight or nine years came into the shop with her father. She proffered me a pile of about ten paperback children's books and asked if I'd like to buy them, whilst her father stood behind at some distance, supervising. It was evident to me that the father saw this as some sort of rite of passage for his daughter, so I felt only too glad to be able to help.

I looked at the books, which were all in very good condition, and smiled as I offered the girl five pounds.

"Five pounds!" exclaimed the father, suddenly springing forward. "I don't think so!"

"Is there a problem?" I asked.

"Yes!" he fumed. "I'm a businessman myself and I just know that it's not enough."

"Well," I said, outwardly calm, "I have a means by which I can calculate the value of the books to *me*, so presumably you have some sort of system for calculating their worth to *you*?"

"Yes," he answered, but rather unconvincingly.

"Then would you like to tell me what your system is?" I asked.

"No."

"So what you are telling me is... you *have* a system for calculating the worth of these books, but you're not prepared to tell me what it is — is that right?"

"Yes."

"Well, what I am going to suggest is that you take these books and hawk them around as many second-hand bookshops as you possibly can until you get a better price than I've offered. And when you do, I want you to promise to come back to tell me where that shop is so that I can sell *my* books to them as well!"

An hour or so later I decided to go to the door to get a little air, when who should I bump into but the businessman and his daughter.

"Well?" I asked. "How did you get on?"

"Look," he replied contritely, "I owe you an apology. I'm sorry, I was completely out of order."

He wouldn't tell me what they got for them, but they ended up selling their books to another shop in the town, where I know with certainty that they would not have been offered more than a pound.

What puzzled me was why he was prepared to part with the books for a relative pittance, knowing that it was such an ungenerous offer, especially after giving me such a hard time over mine.

Whatever the reason, if the purpose of the exercise had been to instruct his daughter on how to engage in a successful business transaction, then it had badly backfired on him.

But at least he apologised.

I paid as much as I could for stock in the belief that by word of mouth it would encourage a good, regular supply; but, no matter how good the rate offered, some people were not happy.

One man offered me a bag of books, which I looked through and then offered fifteen pounds for.

"Is that the best you can do?" he asked in disappointed disgust.

"Look, try Smithfield with them," I suggested.

"I've just come from there," he replied.

"And what did you *they* offer you?"

"Three pounds."

"So fifteen pounds it is, then?" I ventured.

It was.

Much of the stock I bought over the years was acquired from 'call-outs' to houses around the country, and some areas proved more fruitful than others.

The territory of the Ballymena Scot was generally not a happy hunting ground for me. No matter how good a price I offered for the books it was apparently never quite enough, and I invariably left empty-handed.

On one call near Kells, an old farmer met me at the farmhouse and took me along a little lane to his sister's house, which was situated in some beautifully tree-lined surroundings. He explained on the way how she had been a great lover of books, but recent circumstances had necessitated her being admitted to a home.

On entering the front door I was confronted by shelves of books lining the vestibule walls, and I immediately set to work in earnest; but, every time I lifted a book for closer examination, the farmer was peering right over my shoulder asking — "Is thon a guid yin?" (is that a good one?), *i.e.* was it worth anything. This continued into the living room and all round the ground floor until I'd completed my assessment there.

"There's mair abin," he announced at that point, meaning that there were more to be seen upstairs. Thankfully he let me go up alone, so I was able to look at those books without interference, but the upshot was that you would have struggled to assemble a more worthless collection of printed matter if you'd been trying.

He intercepted me on the way back downstairs and asked me straight out what I'd offer him for them.

"Nothing," I said bluntly.

He smiled as though he understood this to be part of my bargaining strategy.

"Awa' wi' ye," he said. "What's tha best ye can dae?"

"Nothing," I repeated. "In fact, you'd have to pay *me* to take them away.

At first he was unsure of how to take this, but when it finally registered with him that I was perfectly serious, his whole mien changed instantly. Once he realised there was no haggling to be done, the man visibly relaxed and invited me back to the farmhouse for a cup of tea and a bite to eat, where he and his wife chatted merrily with me for some time.

"Your sister must have been some reader in her day," I said to him as I sipped my tea.

"Ah, the poor craytur," he answered. "She cudnae read wan wurd, no yin." (She couldn't read a word, not one).

"She wusnae a' there," he explained, tapping his right temple with his finger, "but ye cudnae cum tae tha hoose wi'oot a book in yer haun, if ye wanted tae please her."

A successful buying expedition could often lead to referrals.

In one case I was called out by the headmaster of Sullivan Upper Grammar School in Holywood, County Down.

He had already been in touch with at least two other dealers who felt it wasn't worth their while to go out to have a look at what he had.

The books, in fairness, wouldn't have been of enormous interest to most booksellers from here as the bulk were English history books for which there wasn't a particularly strong local market.

Nevertheless, they were good histories, and with there being the odd Irish-interest item amongst them, I made him an offer which he graciously accepted.

The two of us had got on well and I have to say that he was a gentleman with whom it was a pleasure to do business.

A few weeks later I received a telephone call from a friend of his who taught at Campbell College in Belfast. He was selling up to go to live in Donegal and had a few books which he wanted to offload.

He arranged to see me at my house and brought in several boxes of books for me to look through. Most of them were pretty run-of-the-mill shelf-fillers, but one volume particularly attracted my attention, and it happened to be a Mills & Boon publication!

Mills & Boon hadn't always just produced cheap paperback romance novels, and this was a hardback copy of what I suspected to be the first English edition of *The Phantom of the Opera* by Gaston Leroux.

"Look," I said, "leave this one with me and I'll do a little research into it and get back to you."

As it turned out it *was* the first English edition of 1911 and we agreed that I would put it on sale for £250 and that we would split the money if it sold. It did, and we did.

Some months later again, he gave me a ring to say that his aunt was downsizing house in Ballymoney and asked me if I'd like to come to look at *her* books.

The hallway and a back room were lined with shelves holding several hundred books, but they weren't of great quality, and I remember feeling really awkward about the thought of having to make an offer for them. There were so many books and yet they were worth so little, less than a hundred pounds, making it difficult for me to come out of this with my reputation intact.

Then, as I ambled about thinking about what I was going to say, I was shown into another room in which sat a cardboard box full of old leather bindings. These turned out to be some very scarce eighteenth and nineteenth century Irish histories, so I was able to offer a four figure sum for the whole collection, an offer which was duly accepted.

The car was completely filled to the roof that day and I remember being in fear of the suspension collapsing on the way back to Bangor.

That was not the end of the run though.

A while later the aunt's friend was moving to England and she also called me out to look at the books she wished to dispose of.

On this occasion I politely declined the majority of books as they were of a religious nature, not my speciality, but I did get some good local histories.

That one call to Sullivan Upper had directly generated three other successful deals.

An old school friend gave me another referral which I was somewhat reticent to take. I was informed that the parents of a friend of hers wanted rid of some books which were kept in their pantry. From the little I had been told, I had reservations about the quantity and quality of the books on offer, but I went nevertheless.

The house was on an avenue which lay between the Malone Road and Lisburn Road in Belfast, and I was welcomed in by the husband and wife.

In my mind, a pantry was a place to keep food and no more than a couple of feet deep, but this was an older house with one which stretched back over twelve feet, and the whole of it was literally crammed solid with books.

It took me hours to pull them all out and sort through them.

The books were all in great order and mostly very sellable, so I made an offer of some hundreds and saw immediately that the husband and wife were a bit taken aback.

"Maybe I shouldn't tell you this," said the wife, "but we were going to pay someone to take them away."

"That makes no difference to me," I replied. "I'd have still offered you the same even if I'd known."

"But do you never make mistakes?" she asked.

"Certainly, I do," I said, "but I haven't in this case."

"Sure?"

"Sure!"

The books took quite a few car loads to shift over a two day period, and I was pretty tired at the end of it all.

When I thought that the job was complete and was about to say my goodbyes, I was told that those books had only been the tip of the iceberg.

I was taken upstairs to the landing, the attic hatch was opened, and a folding ladder dropped down.

Climbing to the top and peering into the loft, my eyes were confronted with sacks and loose piles of books jammed tight to the rafters in every direction.

I clambered in and took an hour or two to make an assessment from the sample batch nearest to me.

The collection would cost me thousands, but it was well worth having, so I made an offer which wasn't accepted without argument. These good people were reluctant to take so much money from me, and it took some effort to persuade them that I knew what I was doing.

This time I had to hire a van and bring a couple of helpers, my elder son and his friend. The sacks were heavy and very dusty, and had to be lowered from the attic with great care, then carried downstairs and loaded into the van. It was back-breaking work and the three of us were dirtier than nineteenth century street urchins in no time at all.

It took several days and quite a few van journeys to clear that attic, and I found myself quite sorry when it was.

I had enjoyed the company of this couple and had taken many a pleasant tea break with them, helping the wife with her cryptic crossword for the day.

The husband had spent his lifetime collecting these books together, and it must have been a terrible wrench for him to part with them after all this time, practical as the decision might have been.

Some of the books dated from his army days during the Second World War, and included guides for the British soldier on how to conduct himself amongst the local populace in various foreign places. Others predated the war and had obviously been in his family for several generations.

Buying books did have its poignant side at times.

The biggest collection I ever bought was that of a deceased clergyman whose books had been stored untouched for years in a massive unused hall in a school. The boxes were piled high and took up more than half the space in that great hall.

It took me a solid week with the aid of several helpers to transport that collection in a van to storage I had rented just outside Groomsport. There must have been easily over 20,000 volumes and many of those books still lie there unprocessed to this day. I begin to wonder now if I'll ever manage to find time to sort through them all before I myself shed this mortal coil.

This was a truly eclectic collection, with books on a myriad of subjects, and dating back as early as the sixteenth century.

I bought it for a five figure sum in conjunction with a fellow bookseller and long-time friend. In terms of sales that was the best year I ever had.

My presence was once requested by two brothers who were clearing out their father's flat in Knocknagoney, near Holywood, County Down.

Judging from his books, the father had been a well-read, self-educated man, the type of man for whom I have the greatest admiration.

I bought what I could, but there was a residue of classic novels and plays, encyclopaedias, outdated dictionaries and other reference material which had now virtually no resale value.

"What do you suggest we do with them?" asked one of the brothers. "Should we just put them in the skip we've hired?"

It went against the grain for me to say that directly, but I indicated that there was really no sensible alternative. They would only be wasting their time trying to get money for them from the book trade and libraries and charity shops weren't likely to benefit from them much either.

The next afternoon I received a telephone enquiry in the shop.

"Do you buy books, mate?"

"Yes," I said, "depending on what they are."

"I've got a whole clatter of different ones here," the man informed me. "Story books, dictionaries, encyclopaedias — I've even got one with a signed photograph of Shakespeare in the front!"

"You wouldn't happen to be ringing from Knocknagoney, by any chance?" I asked.

There was a short silence before the puzzled would-be vendor asked — "Yes, but how did *you* know?"

"Just a wild guess," I replied.

I was often plagued by lay experts when it came to buying books. Too many people had distant cousins or friendly neighbours who by some arcane process had acquired the knowledge which allowed them to attach a value to a collection of books without having any experience in the trade whatsoever.

At a house in Carrickfergus on one occasion, I was presented with the biggest load of unsellable rubbish I'd seen in a long time, but it was rubbish for which the lady of the house seemed to hold great expectations.

Normally I didn't ask people what they wanted for their books as I believed that it was my job as the expert to give *them* a quotation and, if it wasn't acceptable, then they could try elsewhere to get more. In this case, however, paying a penny for them would have been a penny wasted, but I was curious to know what was on her mind.

"How much were you expecting to get for these?" I asked.

"Well," she said, "Mr McWilliams down the street says that I shouldn't accept any less than three hundred pounds for them."

I then suggested that she should sell them to Mr McWilliams for two hundred pounds and allow the man to make a good commission by selling them on. I thought it only right that he should benefit from his extensive knowledge of books.

Selling Books

Some sales have stuck in my mind over the years because of their unusual nature.

For a short time I had a friend's mother assisting me in the shop, and on her first day she pointed to a coffee-table biography of the actress Julie Christie and said — "That's a lovely book."

"Yes," I said, "but I'll guarantee you that it'll still be here in a year's time."

The next person through the door lifted and bought it.

This was not an uncommon phenomenon. It seemed uncanny at times, but just by thinking about or handling a book it could bring about a sale the same day. Many times I have looked at books which had been with me a long time and thought 'It's a wonder that nobody has bought that,' only to have someone purchase it within hours.

I'm unable to tell you the title of another memorable sale I made.

In supplementing my income by doing milk rounds at night I often fell asleep in the bookshop during the day. Sometimes I would wake to the tail end of one of my snores and slowly focus on someone standing in front of me, waiting to be served.

On one occasion, however, I opened my eyes simply to see a little pile of coins placed neatly on the edge of the counter.

My elder boy would have been about five or six years at the time and was in the shop playing with a toy on the floor.

A man had spent some time leafing through a book, when suddenly my son got up, walked over, and placed himself between the reader and the shelves. He looked up at him and asked:

"Are you going to buy that book? My Daddy needs the money!"

This didn't actually lead to a sale as it happened, but it was a valiant effort, worthy of note.

Often time was at such a premium that I didn't always have the opportunity to properly research books which came in to stock. This was in the pre-Internet days when the only option was to plough through numerous magazines, catalogues, and volumes of the *Book Auction Records* in the hope of finding the information I was after. So, occasionally, I would just take a risk and make an educated guess.

I did this with the *Golfing Annual* of 1888, pricing it at twenty-five pounds and putting it on sale.

Shortly afterwards a man approached me with the book in his hand and asked — "What's the best you can do?"

"Twenty-five pounds," I replied.

"But it's already twenty-five pounds," he moaned.

"I know," I said, "and it's probably worth a lot more than that."

He pushed and he pressed for a discount, but I absolutely refused to budge, until he eventually gave up and left the shop in a rather disgruntled manner.

Within the hour he was back, red-faced, out of breath, and dripping with sweat. He lifted the book again and handed it to me with twenty-five pounds in notes, and this time there was no attempt at bartering.

He said nothing, but left the shop in a lot less of a rush than he'd come in, wiping his brow as he went.

It was several months later that I stumbled across it valued at £300-500 in the *Book and Magazine Collector*.

My educated guess just wasn't quite educated enough on that occasion.

The manager of a Belfast hotel came to me one day and asked if I could supply him with a thousand hardback books for decoration of the bar.

"No problem," I said. "When do you want them for?"

"Tomorrow."

We struck a deal for about thirty pence a head and I got the books ready for collection the next day.

Some time afterwards I heard that the shelves in the bar had been made too narrow and that the books had to be taken to a saw-mill to have their tops cut off.

This bar, I thought, would be a veritable paradise for those who could only ever manage to read half a book.

Another sale was memorable simply because it was the most expensive.

Part of the deceased clergyman's collection I bought included a three volume edition of Plato's works, published in 1578.

I got five thousand pounds for that.

It was sold to an Irish book collector who worked as a financial executive in the City of London.

He filled his house so full of books that he eventually had to buy another to live in.

A third house was required a few years later.

Amongst the other notable sales from that same collection was a sixteen volume set of Shakespeare's plays and poems, edited by Edmond Malone, an Irish Shakespearean scholar, and published in Dublin, Ireland, in 1794. The set was sold to a lady in Dublin, California, in the United States of America, for £875.

Characters

For some reason, second-hand bookshops seem to attract more than their fair share of characters and eccentrics. I would almost dare say that there is more eccentricity per square foot in a used bookshop on a given day than in any other business in the same town or city.

'Big Henry' would spend his days frequenting libraries and bookshops in Belfast. Nobody knew his source of income or very much about him at all, but he always seemed to be wandering about with a large brown envelope tucked under his arm, the significance of which never came to light.

He would use my stock as his own to quote to other booksellers via the *Bookdealer* and other trade magazines, but pretend that he was having the books held over for 'friends'. Unfortunately, my organisational skills were found wanting at times and the books would frequently get mislaid or sold, leaving Henry to explain himself to his friends. If he'd just been open and honest with me about his little sideline I'd have happily helped him all I could. But Henry thought himself a lot smarter than he actually was, and suffered the consequences.

Henry was a well-built chap who always sported a 'short back and sides' haircut, and his bearing was reminiscent of a military man or police officer, although I don't believe he had ever been either.

He had a habit of leaning against a person's shoulder and speaking to them out of the side of his mouth in a very secret service kind of a way, even if he was only imparting his latest assessment of the weather.

At times he would rub me up the wrong way and we had squared up to each other on several occasions, although we never came to blows. He liked to physically domineer people, giving the impression that he was a particularly tough individual who was not to be messed with.

I, however, believed that beneath the tough exterior lay a rampant coward just waiting to get out, and I hatched a plan to prove it.

Henry would come in to the shop every Saturday and leave his bits and pieces in my safe-keeping whilst he took a tour of the town.

On one particular Saturday he returned to find me standing behind the counter rubbing my chin and looking inordinately worried.

"What's the matter with you?" he asked with genuine concern.

"Och, nothing," I said, "nothing much."

"There's obviously something bothering you," he replied. "What is it?"

He kept pursuing the question until he eventually got it out of me how, in his absence, a couple of hoodlums had been in the shop causing a nuisance of themselves and I'd unceremoniously had to get rid of them.

"But they said they'd be back later with the rest of the squad," I told him.

"Well then," said Henry, "my advice would be to close the shop and get yourself away home."

I explained that I couldn't do that when people might be making special journeys to the shop expecting me to be open and, apart from that, if I didn't face up to the thugs now I'd probably only be deferring the problem to a later date.

"No," I continued, "my thinking is that if *you* stayed here with me, the two of us could see these gangsters off once and for all."

The colour in Henry's face seemed to drain instantaneously. He didn't make any reply, but wandered off to the far end of the shop in a very pensive state.

After a while he came back and repeated his previous advice, only this time there was a hint of desperation in his voice.

Again I refused to take it, but insisted that with him beside me I would have no qualms about facing whatever came through the door.

As closing time approached, Henry became more and more agitated, constantly checking his watch, until he could hold out no longer. With five minutes to go, he approached the last remaining customer and unilaterally informed the poor bewildered woman that she had to leave immediately as the shop was shutting. He ushered her to the door with great haste.

He could scarcely wait for me to switch the lights off and lock that shop door, then he was off in a flash in the opposite direction to me.

Some months later I was sitting in the shop when 'Murphy', another regular who hadn't been about for a while, came in and announced that he'd heard all about me.

"Oh?" I said. "Do tell!"

Well, apparently I had been taking an awful hammering on the street by a gang of thugs when, luckily, Big Henry happened to be passing, grabbed them by the collars and threw them into the air one by one, before sending them all packing with a flea in the ear.

Murphy had heard the story from another bookseller twenty miles away, who had heard it from someone else, who had heard it from someone else. But there was only one possible source for this tale of heroism in the face of these imaginary thugs!

I never told Big Henry how I had set him up, nor mentioned the report I received of his self-fabricated bravery. My intention was not to humiliate him, but to prove to myself that my theory was correct and gain a little amusement from it at the same time. Much as he irritated me at times, I actually liked the great lump, and when I heard some years ago that he had died alone and unexpectedly, with no family to mourn him, a terrible sadness came over me.

He was a good, kind, friendly big man, who loved his books, and I regret that I'll not have the opportunity to joust with him again.

He was a character.

Murphy was a loose cannon who drove fear into the hearts of most booksellers in the country. He wasn't violent or threatening, but inclined to create havoc and mayhem wherever he went. He was not to be bound by convention.

I have heard that he once borrowed a car and, finding himself stuck in a traffic jam, abandoned it in the queue with the engine still running, then went about his business as usual and without a care.

He would appear in the shop after long absences, usually the worse for drink, and entertain the customers with very dramatic recitals of Yeats' poems, taking long theatrical puffs on his cigarette between verses.

Frequently he arrived with quantities of books which he made his mission to sell, and I suspect that other booksellers donated these as a means to get rid of him, for Murphy had a habit of turning up at their homes completely uninvited.

Sadly, I came too late on the scene to witness Murphy's heyday, but one story which was related to me will give an idea of why he became such a legend and figure of fear in the world of second-hand books.

Murphy did not suffer the pretentious gladly and took great delight in devising plans to ridicule them. His target on one particular occasion was a lady book and print seller who thought more highly of herself than was perhaps justified.

He telephoned her from another bookseller's shop, using a fake name, to offer her his late father's most excellent and valuable collection of books — books which, according to Murphy, had been acquired over a lifetime from the most prestigious of dealers and auction houses.

Murphy insisted that his accomplice bookseller listen in to the conversation on a phone extension, and then proceeded to deride and denigrate him to his prey, saying that he wouldn't even consider offering the books to such an ignoramus. She willingly took the bait and added voluminously to the character assassination, with the upshot being that Murphy would give her first refusal.

As soon as he put the phone down, Murphy asked the bookseller to collect together all the junk that he wanted to get rid off, whilst he went off to organise a van.

When he was sure that she was out, Murphy drove to the lady's house and dumped a van load of the most worthless volumes imaginable in her driveway.

Then he waited a few months.

Murphy liked to play the long game and knew that the dealer would keep the books only so long before having to dispose of them. In the belief that she had already done so, he telephoned again to ask what she was prepared to offer him for his father's valuable collection.

You can imagine his horror and indignation when he was informed that his pater's cherished books had been so unceremoniously dumped, and he advised her that vigorous legal action would follow.

I have no doubt that the poor lady would have suffered a few restless nights in the subsequent weeks.

Stories of Murphy's antics are legion, and if ever the Irish booksellers could exchange notes, a volume could be devoted to him entirely.

He was an extraordinarily intelligent man, with easily the sharpest mind I have ever encountered, and I suspect that much of his wayward behaviour was born of ennui.

Murphy also died relatively young and unexpectedly.

There was a middle-aged lady who used to be seen wandering all around Bangor, always wearing green Wellington boots and a long woollen scarf. Her hair was frizzy and long, and usually held in place at the back with a clip.

She would occasionally come in to buy a book for fifty pence from my bargain bin, but would never speak.

Only on one occasion did she quietly ask if I could hold a book over for her.

"Yes, certainly," I said. "Whose name shall I put on it?"

She replied so softly that I could not make out what she had said, so I asked her if she would mind repeating herself.

The second time I thought I heard a barely audible 'Christmas Eve'.

That is the name I attached to the book.

Later I discovered that she had given the same name to another shopkeeper in the town.

Had this been a pet name her father or mother had used for her when she was young? Or did that day signify some turning point in her life? Who knows.

On walking down a Bangor street one day I spotted a book she had bought from me propped up in a bedsit window, faded by the sun.

I remember feeling particularly sorry for her at that moment. She always gave me the impression that she had come from a 'good' background, and I wondered what had brought her to this, living alone in bedsit land.

One day the verger of the Parish Church was cleaning the porch when he noticed one copper coin after another being slid across the floor from under the door. He opened it to discover Christmas Eve kneeling on the other side.

"What are you doing, love?" he asked her.

"I'm just giving these to God so he won't forget me," she replied.

I haven't seen her for many years now, but the elderly church member and life-long book collector who recently related this story assures me that Christmas Eve is still to be seen walking the streets of Bangor in her green Wellington boots and long woollen scarf.

The Bookshop Window

The little Bangor bookshop was not on a main thoroughfare and business could be very slow at times. In fact, I remember at one period not taking any money at all for two days in a row, which was rather depressing. The third day was only marginally better, but at least it wasn't another duck.

Often, to relieve the boredom between customers, when I'd had enough of reading, I would gaze out of the shop window and follow the journeys of the few passers-by and watch the traffic moving up and down the street.

This occasionally brought its rewards.

One day I saw a little hatchback car come to an abrupt halt on the hill, and a police car with flashing blue lights pull up a few yards behind. Two angry-looking police officers jumped out, promptly put their hats on, and approached the pursued vehicle with some purpose in their step.

As they did so, a flustered middle-aged lady of generous proportions struggled free of her little car.

Unfortunately, she neglected to apply the handbrake properly.

There was a bit of a thud and the sound of breaking glass as the pilotless police car got shunted several feet backwards.

If the policemen were angry before, they were absolutely livid now. They quickly examined the damage, then began marching up and down in a most animated manner, à la Keystone Cops, whilst directing some carelessly chosen words of wisdom towards their horrified captive.

This was great entertainment, entirely free, and the variety of expression on the three actors' faces made for great comedy.

I don't know what the poor lady had done to trigger the pursuit, but I imagine that it was more likely to have been a traffic-related offence than armed robbery.

Through that window I also watched a heated exchange between a man and woman who were standing beside a very plush BMW. Now, when I say it was a heated *exchange*, it was more a case of her being heated and him giving very little in exchange. And when I say *standing*, he was rooted to the spot whilst she marched briskly backwards and forwards, gesticulating angrily and brandishing some sort of metal implement in her hand.

For a moment I feared she would strike him with it, but there was something even more horrible on her mind.

Coming to the front of the car, she swung that metal bar for all she was worth, smashing one headlight and then the other. This done, she turned her attention to the windscreen, which proved a little obstinate for a few blows, but the lady was not for turning and pursued her objective with vigour until the mission was satisfactorily accomplished.

She took a short break from her task to further unburden her mind to her petrified foil, before returning to polish off the two wing mirrors.

In minutes she had systematically smashed every bit of glass in the car and, for a finale, rendered several emphatic strikes to the roof.

He'd not forget *her* birthday again in a hurry, I thought.

That bookshop window featured in my decision to finally close the doors of the business and work from home.

Much as I loved the wee shop and had done my utmost to keep it going, I really wasn't getting any financial benefit from it. The landlord was getting his rent, the council was getting its rates, and the few customers were getting some great book bargains. I, however, was only getting the headaches associated with running a shop.

Nevertheless, I probably would have kept going for a while longer if it hadn't have been for the IRA bomb of March 1993, which devastated Bangor.

Up to that point the 'Troubles' hadn't directly impacted on my business. Belfast had been dark and depressing in winter evenings, the city virtually deserted by 6 pm, and periodically my journeys to and from the shop would have been delayed by bomb alerts and other incidents, but generally life went on as normal.

Our little terraced house in Bangor was just one street away from the shop, and I woke that night to feel and see the whole bedroom shaking. I was temporarily disorientated and, not understanding what was happening, momentarily felt my time had come.

When the shock had passed and I realised that a bomb had gone off, I got dressed and walked down to the shop. The large plate glass window had been completely blown in and the books peppered with tiny fragments of glass.

I walked to the top of the street to survey the damage to the rest of the town, and a combined feeling of sadness, incomprehension and disgust came over me.

If memory serves me correctly, I was told by someone that amongst the injuries that night, some poor young police officer had lost her foot.

My wife also got injured when part of the bedroom ceiling collapsed, badly cutting her face, but thankfully no serious or permanent damage was done.

Nevertheless, I had to go out and do a milk round that night as normal.

Whilst waiting for compensation for the damage, I had to pay for a replacement window myself, which further added to the financial strain. Many of the books, for which I didn't get compensated, had to be dumped because it was impossible to be sure that they were entirely free of small fragments of glass.

This was basically the straw that broke the camel's back. I decided then that it didn't make sense to keep the bookshop going. If I'd actually been making a good income from it, then it may have been a different story, but Bangor had been attacked the previous year as well and there were no guarantees that it wouldn't be hit again. I just couldn't afford to suffer such setbacks on top of everything else, so I saw out the few remaining months of my lease, then closed the shop door for good.

Valedictory

That old double-fronted shop in Belfast, scene of my bookselling apprenticeship, is no more. The block on which it stood was levelled to the ground and a building of modern utilitarian blandness erected in its place. The little shop in Bangor, a one-time converted terraced house, has so far avoided the wave of architectural vandalism which has swept the country in recent years. Not so fortunate was the Victorian railway station at the top of the street with its charming stone-faced clock tower. It was supplanted by a great glass monstrosity to which time can add no character.

Now, do not think me a type of contemporary Luddite, opposed to all modernity and change. When I closed my shop I began to work from home, selling mainly by catalogue and at bookfairs, but as the Internet developed I embraced the opportunity to sell online and, in 1997, I believe I became the first secondhand bookseller in Northern Ireland, possibly the whole of Ireland, to build an online bookstore. Thereafter, however, there developed a number of small independent book marketplaces which quickly got swallowed one by the other, until today most dealers are highly dependent on selling their books through a handful of big virtual stores which attract customers by the enormous range of stock they can offer. As these megasites move steadily towards an effective monopoly, this increasingly gives them the power to dictate their cut and the terms of sale to the booksellers.

The advent of the Internet certainly gave booksellers the opportunity to sell to a world market, but the obverse of that is that it also exposed them to massive competition. As the big online book marketplaces grew, they sought to boost their size and revenue by making it easy for anyone to sell books on their sites. This had the effect of driving prices down to a point where at one stage it looked as though books were to be offered for nothing, or even minus figures, the sellers banking on making a small margin from postage and packaging charges. Not a bad thing you might think, but it did have its consequences — it made a lot of books worthless when they came to be sold. What I had paid someone five pounds for in the past I could no longer afford to risk buying at any price, knowing that there were likely to be numerous other copies on sale across the world for pennies, and generally its the cheapest price which wins.

Another effect of this vast marketplace and these ultra-cheap prices is that a large percentage of second-hand bookshops around the world have been put out of business, and those booksellers who have transferred to selling online are finding it increasingly difficult to compete with the thousands of dabblers and hobbyists who have acquired a little stock for buttons, or sell their own books for a bit of fun — and no one can blame them for that. Neither can the new breed of volume sellers who are in it entirely for money and view books simply as units of sale be condemned for trying to earn a crust, but I worry that professionals with years of experience and knowledge of books will be driven to move out of the trade altogether.

It used to be that most people coming into the second-hand book trade did so through a deep love of books, and were prepared to invest capital in stock, shelving and in renting or buying a shop. They acquired knowledge through experience and were in a position to inform and advise customers. Now, not just in the world of books, but in most other retail and service sectors as well, it seems harder to find people who know their business and are competent enough to deal with queries. And it all seems so much more impersonal now as well.

Changes in the nature of the buyer too seem to have evolved rapidly over the last two decades.

When I first began in the business there were many ardent, often compulsive collectors who constantly did the rounds to see what they might pick up in their field of interest. There were lots of local historians, for example, who would compete with each other to be first to something scarce, so those books rarely lasted a week on the shelves. Gradually those men — for they were, inexplicably, all men — began to die off, and not a single young collector of the same ilk came through to replace them. It is now not uncommon for me to have those same scarce items on the shelves for *years*, even at a lower absolute price than they were twenty years ago. These men knew their books and subject matter well, and were extremely creative in inventing new ways to sneak yet more books past their wives.

I confess that I cannot explain what brought about this rapid decline in the number of collectors. No doubt it will be as a result of a complex combination of social factors, but perhaps the growth of so many competing forms of entertainment played a major role. Homes, too, seem now to be ultra clean and furnished in a more minimalist fashion, legislating against the display of dusty old books.

Another blow to my enjoyment of the business is the imminent forced closure of the little village post office in Groomsport, with its hand-painted wooden sign above the door and red pillar box outside. The windowsill sits only inches above the pavement and sports several short fleur-de-lys-shaped metal prongs to which customers would tether their dogs whilst they went in to buy their stamps or post their parcels. I have used that post office for thirteen years, holding complete faith in the honesty and ability of the postmaster who was always pleased to handle the parcels from my mail order business. I would leave him with a bundle of cash to process my sacks of post at his leisure, knowing that it would be done with perfect competence.

Royal Mail decided to dispose of thousands of local post office franchises around the country in an effort to 'improve' the service to its customers. I fear the improvement for many sole traders like me will mean standing in a long queue, probably within a busy supermarket, waiting to be served by an ill-trained and indifferent paid employee who will roll his or her eyes at the sight of a sack of parcels.

Change is obviously only progress if it meets with my approval, and things are unlikely to improve significantly until the world has fallen under my benign*ish* dictatorship. If that doesn't happen then, looking on the bright side, I'll be dead soon enough and won't have to suffer this brave new world too much longer.

Wink.

*"'Tis pleasant, sure, to see one's name in print;
A book's a book, altho' there's nothing in't."*

Lord Byron

"The book salesman should be honored because he brings to our attention, as a rule, the very books we need most and neglect most."

Frank Crane